Do You Have a Pit Bull Attitude?
Published by
Doug Giles Productions
P.O. Box 800554
Aventura, FL 33280

ISBN: 0-9667501-0-1

Printed in the United States of America
October 1998

Unless otherwise noted, all scripture quotations are from the *King James Bible*. Public Domain.

Editor: Penny Phillips
All illustrations: Doug Giles
Cover and inside layout and design:
Kerry Phillips/kmfillips@mailexcite.com

Dedication

I would like to
dedicate this book to
Homey, Jabbok, Colby,
Bugsy and Beastie—
Pit and Staffy Bulls
who have taught me
more about
persistence, passion,
pleasure and poise
than any human
being I have ever met.

D. Giles~10/98

Do You Have a Pit Bull Attitude?

This book is for my beautiful girls, Hannah and Regis, with my sincere hope that they will always be determined to win the important battles in their lives.

It is also for Mary Margaret, who has helped me through a number of wars in my life and has always pointed out to me when I was acting like a Poodle instead of a Pit Bull.

Do You Have a
Pit Bull
Attitude?

Disclaimer

This book is not an endorsement of the illegal sport of dog fighting. Its content isn't taken from personal experience, either. Though my politically correct buddies may wince a bit at my audacity in using the Pit Bull as my protagonist, I chose this great canine and his laudable traits because he embodies the kind of attitude that success in any field demands. This book is for people who play to win or those who want to become people who play to win, because the Pit Bull symbolizes single-minded persistence. Readers will appreciate utilizing the "Pit Bull Attitude" if they have the old-fashioned chutzpah that it takes to do anything worth being mentioned.

I want to define a few terms used in *Pit Bull Attitude*. First, references to "fighting," "battles," "war," etc. are to be read as metaphors for competition in whatever field you're in. Second, "fighting" in *Pit Bull Attitude* is synonymous with competing honorably. It doesn't imply destroying the competition. Finally, "victory," "rule" and "conquer" mean successfully completing your purpose, goals and the tasks at hand.

Table of Contents

It is surmounting difficulties that makes heroes.

~Louis Kossuth

The Greatest Dog In the World.

> "The American Pit Bull Terrier can do anything any other dog can do and then whip him as well."
>
> ~John Colby

The Pit Bull is one of the most awesome animals on the planet. This book that you have in your hands shows why he is so incredible and why you should seek to be like him. The United States of America thought that the Pit Bull was great enough to be our representative during the first World War. The U.S. didn't choose a Poodle, Chihuahua or a Maltese to represent us. They chose the greatest dog to represent the greatest country—as a symbol to the other countries of who we are and what they would be messing with. During WWI, *Life* magazine frequently had Pit Bulls on their cover and in their cartoons, using them as a symbol of America's stalwart spirit. In Jacqueline O'neil's book, *The American Pit Bull Terrier*, she brings out the fact that the Pit Bull named "Stubby" was the war's outstanding canine soldier. He earned the rank of Sergeant, was mentioned in official dispatches and earned two medals—one for warning of a gas attack and the other for holding a German spy at Chemin des Dames until the American troops arrived.

The Pit Bull was also one of our nation's beloved canine movie stars. Remember the *Our Gang and The Little Rascals* comedy series with Spanky, Alfalfa, Darla and Buck Wheat? Do you remember their dog, Pete? He was a Pit Bull. Did he eat any of the children on T.V.? No. Was he cool, tolerant and well-behaved as the Little Rascals used him to pull their wagons, do their tricks and run their errands? Yep.

This dog rocks. You were made to rock as well. It seems, though, more and more people are getting weak and becoming too soft and are leaning more towards being a Poodle rather than a Pit Bull. We need more Pit Bulls. We need Pit Bull dads, moms, sons, daughters, schools, neighborhoods, businesses, politicians, preachers, teachers, cities, states and nations. We need a Planet Pit Bull. There are too, too many Poodles out there. We need Pit Bull people who have a strong resolve to please their owner—God, who have naturally protective instincts, who are highly trainable, robust and energetic.

You were made for success. You were created in the image of the Greatest Pit Bull...the Pit Bull of Pit Bulls. You are intended to rule and conquer. Don't be a sappy, temperamental, weak, insipid and scared Poodle. Be a Pit Bull. The qualities of the bulldog described in these pages are to be added into your character. Don't just read to read. Read and imitate. And if you don't get it the first time, read it again. Just like shampooing—lather, rinse and repeat...until you cleanse yourself from being a Poodle.

Here's a list of a few famous owners of the Pit Bull:

Fred Astaire • James Caan • Jack Dempsey • Thomas Edison • Michael J. Fox • Helen Keller • Pres. Theodore Roosevelt • Sir Walter Scott • Jan Michael Vincent • Doug Giles

1
Don't Be A Poodle.

If you are looking for an easy way to succeed, for someone to carry you into greatness... you're in for the shock of your life. It is not out there. And if you think it's going to be easy, you're about to have your rose-colored glasses removed, snapped in two and stomped into the ground—which, hopefully, will improve your vision. There is no easy road to a successful family, career or life. The road

Undertake something
that is difficult; it
will do you good.
Unless you try to do
something beyond
what you have
already mastered,
you will never grow.

~Ronald E. Osborne

to success is paved with road kill. The road kill are all the glassy-eyed, weak, unprepared Poodles who're looking for a free ride. But life is a pit fight where only the Pit Bulls survive and thrive. Great accomplishments aren't for the thin-skinned, fearful Poodles. If you are looking for six easy steps to happiness, put this book down and walk slowly away. Greatness is Pit Bull stuff. If you want success, don't be a Poodle.

The only thing easy in life is to follow the crowd. Submit to the norm. That takes no courage. It's easy to do what everyone else does. That's a cinch. That's Poodle stuff. It takes no tenacity. Wienie dogs and fluffy Poodles are experts on the easy things. Mediocrity is easy; yet, the easy is boring. It's easy not to have a dream or a vision. It's easy living for comfort rather than a cause, a purpose, a burning desire, a fight, a chance to prove yourself, slay a dragon, save a nation.

A Poodle wants comfort. A Poodle wants a place next to the A/C with it set on 72 degrees. Poodles love the comfort zone. They hate anything that challenges them to get out of the rut they live in. Poodles think of ease instead of duty. Poodles want a couch rather than a conscience. They want everything on a silver platter. Poodles are only happy when they are comfortable. Pit Bulls are happy when they are engaged in battle. Separate a Pit Bull from a fight, and he'll whine to get back in. Poodles are everywhere; Pit Bulls are rare.

Poodles live for themselves. They want a pillow in their condo and a matching one in their Cadillac. They want caviar. Poodles are non-producers. They contribute nothing… they are nothing. They want to be taken care of… pampered at the salon. They would love nothing more than to have a Poodle-O-Centric universe.

Poodles act as though comfort and luxury were the chief requirements in life, when all that one really needs to be happy is something to be enthused about… something great to live and to die for.

Pit Bulls live for greatness. They live to please their masters. Pits love all people—unless you're a jerk. They have a great sense of discernment that helps them differentiate between a weirdo and a champion. Pits love to fight for audiences. Pit Bulls are hardy, tough, non-finicky dogs who aren't fussy about what they eat or where they sleep. They live for greater things. They live for the master... the people... the battle... the victory.

Does your world revolve around you? Do you look for the path of least resistance? Do you look for the pillow in the Cadillac? Is the comfort zone your focus? If so... you're a Poodle. Is it the battle or the beauty parlor that turns you on? If you have found that you have the above mentioned Poodle traits, drop them now and get a Pit Bull Attitude What you are chasing as a Poodle is boring, low, easy, unfulfilling and ignoble.

Get a Pit Bull vision and a Pit Bull Attitude for something grand. Forget your comfy silk pillow. View your life from the grave, Fi-Fi. Is what you're living for worth dying for? Do you want your tombstone to read, "Here lies Fi-Fi who didn't do anything... a comfort-driven, ease-seeking Poodle"? Or do want to be remembered as a great

Pit Bull with your gravestone reading, "Here lies a summit-or-plummet, shape-up-or-dropout, wholehearted, banzai PIT BULL"?

It's your choice.

Because a fellow has failed once or twice, or a dozen times, you don't want to set him down as a failure till he's dead or loses his courage—and that's the same thing.

~George Horace Lorimer

Pit Bull/ Poodle Test.

2

> **"Examine yourselves, whether ye be in the faith; prove your own selves."**
>
> ~St. Paul

Proceed no farther in this book until you have taken the following test. You must assess your condition before you read any more. You might be a Poodle, and if so, you, your family and your business are in serious trouble. Be raw honest and ruthlessly thorough in your answers to these questions.

Pit Bull Test

- 1. Do you have a definite purpose backed up by a burning desire to see it fulfilled?
- 2. Are you continuously in action working on your plan?
- 3. Is your mind closed towards all negative and discouraging influences from foes, "friends," parents, music, books, tapes, TV, etc.?

o 4. Do you hang out with people who are greater than you in what they have accomplished and who utterly challenge you to excellence?

o 5. Are you self-reliant and independent?

o 6. Do you take responsibility for your life, both failures and successes?

o 7. Do you hate it when you waste time?

o 8. Do you look at life as a game to be played and played like a champion?

o 9. Have you become impervious to the criticisms of small men and women?

o 10. Do you boldly face your fears with faith and move toward your goals?

> **"If you make people think they're thinking, they'll love you. If you really make them think, they'll hate you."**
>
> **~Don Marquis**

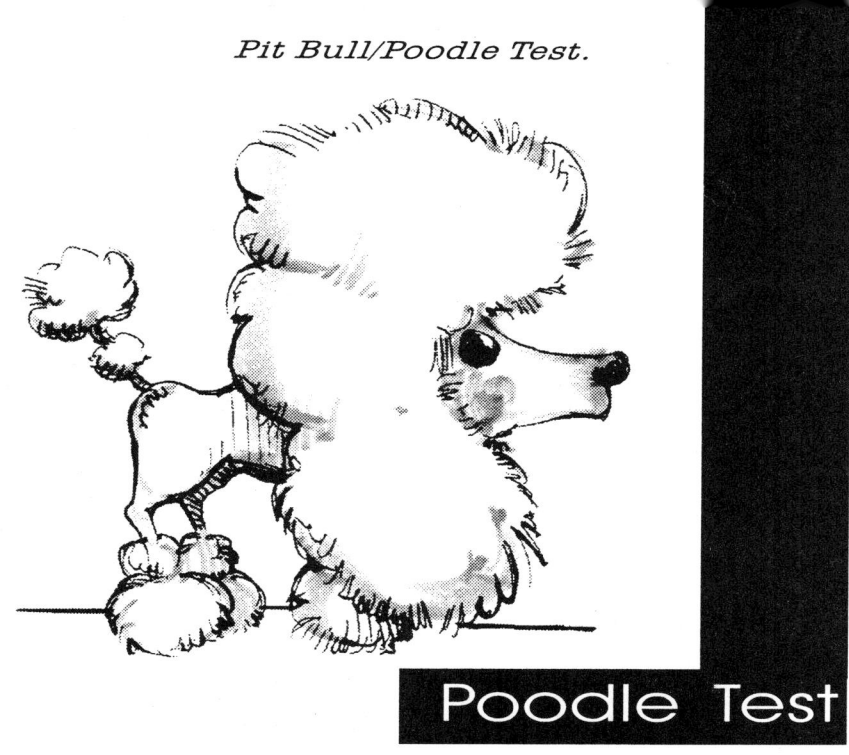

Poodle Test

o 1. Do you complain often?

o 2. Do you avoid association with people greater than you?

o 3. Does your life seem futile and your future hopeless?

o 4. Do you often feel self pity?

o 5. Are you jealous of those who excel you?

o 6. Do you worry a lot?

o 7. Are you overly cautious and negative?

o 8. Are you indifferent and lacking in ambition and enthusiasm?

o 9. Do you constantly use excuses and alibis to explain why you haven't accomplished anything?

o 10. Do you often fantasize about laying on the back dashboard of an air-conditioined Northstar Caddy?

Tally up the checks that were applicable to you in each category. Which one had the majority? If most of the checks fell to the Poodle side, don't close this book. You need it bad. You *can* change. Being a Pit Bull is not chance—it is a choice.

If you checked more in the Pit Bull category, don't close this book, either. Reading it will take off even more flab, making you more fit, giving you a greater edge.

"Why not go out on a limb? Isn't that where the fruit is?"

~Frank Scully

Success Demands a Pit *Bull* *Attitude.*

A determination to succeed is the only way to succeed that I know anything about.

~William Feather

Success demands persistent courage. Calvin Coolidge said, "Nothing in the world can take the place of persistence: Talent will not; nothing is more common than unsuccessful men with talent. Genius will not; unrewarded genius is almost a proverb. Education will not; the world is full of educated derelicts. Persistence and determination alone are omnipotent."

Having a dream is not enough to succeed. Dreaming is easy. Dreamers are more numerous than the hairs on an Amish woman's chin. Dreamers are a dime a dozen. Dreaming is easy; success is tough stuff. The people who succeed are few and far between. What separates the successful from the unsuccessful? What separates the men from the boys...the Arnold Schwarzenegger's from the Michael Jackson's. Is it luck? Chance?

No—it's a Pit Bull Attitude. If you want success in your life… if you want to raise a great family… have an incredible marriage… run a killer business… excel in sports, music, education, politics, the sciences or the arts—you must become a Pit Bull. You cannot be a poodle and succeed. You must be a Pit. A radical, well-bred, deeply game bulldog. If you are not a Pit Bull, life will walk on you. No— it will stomp on you with heavy, construction-grade, steel-toed combat boots… if you don't have the persistence and the determination of the greatest of all dogs—the Pit Bull.

If you have a dream or a vision… if you have something you want to do with your life besides drinking malt liquor, working a crummy job and sitting on your rear watching other people live out their dreams… then you must get an attitude. A dream plus an attitude equals success. But not just any attitude… you need a Pit

Bull Attitude. Pit Bulls epitomize courage and persistence. They are little, scrappy warriors who will not back down. They face difficulties with a win-or-die perspective. They love the battle... they love the heat... they love the fight. Everything that is good, praiseworthy and noble comes through difficulty. Greatness isn't easy. If it were, it wouldn't be greatness—and everyone would be great.

Are you ready to do something with your life? Are you tired of getting whipped and bested by this world and circumstance? Good. It's about time. It's not too late to change, so don't despair. But you must change in a right direction.

Here are five ways to determine whether or not you're ready to change from being a Poodle to a Pit Bull:

1. You're unsatisfied.
2. You have feelings of being

restricted. Nothing works.

3. You're frustrated.
4. You have the feeling of lack. You know there's more to life but you haven't touched it.
5. You have feelings of being useless.

If you're a Poodle, it isn't going to do you any good to turn into a wienie dog. If you want the ultimate life then you must set your sights on personally becoming the ultimate fighting machine—a Pit Bull. Say this with me right now. Come on, shout it out! Don't worry if it scares your Poodle friends. Don't worry if they think you're crazy. Who cares what poodles think? Come on say it—"I am sick of being a poodle! I'm tired of wearing bows and ribbons, having my toenails painted pink and going to dog shows. I'm tired of getting my tail kicked by life. I want to be great! I want to do something besides lay on a frilly pillow! **GOD... MAKE ME A PIT BULL NOW!!!"**

There are some things one can only achieve by a deliberate leap in the opposite direction. One has to go abroad in order to find the home one has lost. ~Franz Kafka

There you go, Sparky... didn't that feel good? Get mad, Dude. It's good for you. You have tolerated mediocrity and nominalism for too long. Now, get rid of every excuse you have for why you aren't a success... for why you are not pursuing your vision. Then, get away from all your Poodle friends who drag you down to their level. Take a deep breath... aah... and get ready to begin to live your dream instead of what this world is dishing out to you.

The first step towards outward achievement is always inward transformation. If you really meant what you just said, the transformation has already begun to take place. You're soon going to begin to find yourself ready to fight in the morning. You're soon going to find yourself being a leader instead of a little Poodle follower. You're now becoming a happy, scrappy, ready-to-face-and-confront-and-conquer-anything-that-walks-crawls-or-flies—you're a Pit Bull. You're not running anymore. You're a lean mean Pit Bull machine. Now, you *must* have success. You *must* do great in school. You *must* excel in business. You *will* have a great family. You *will* get the job or business you have always dreamed of because you have got a Pit Bull Attitude. The common repulses you. The ordinary makes you want to puke. No—you want to win, lead and conquer.

You are one fine animal, you Pit Bull, you. You know life is difficult... but you don't care because you are not just another dog. You not only want to succeed, you *will* succeed—because you actually dig the fight... the whole process of attainment. You are a crazy animal! You really love the battle!

Aggressive fighting for the right is the greatest sport in the world.

~Theodore Roosevelt

Pit Bulls Are 4 Happy.

It takes courage to live—courage and strength and hope and humor...

~Jerome P. Fleishman

Even though you are a Pit Bull... a warrior dog... that doesn't mean you have to act tough. Pit Bulls aren't mean or sullen. They don't walk around the planet carting bags of problems. Pit Bulls are happy. They love life because they know they rule and other dogs drool. They're not victims. You'll never see a Pit

Bull get on *The Ricki Lake Show* and blame other dogs for his life. Pit Bulls live. They don't merely exist—they thrive. They live the now and set their sights on the preferable.

Pit Bulls don't act like wolverines, and they certainly don't pout like a little dejected poodle that didn't get the sqeaky toy it wanted at PetSmart. Pit Bulls are fun to be around. I have never heard a Pit Bull whine—except when it wanted to get into a battle.

The cool thing about Pit Bulls is that they know when to fight and whom to fight and when to chill out. They don't go around starting fights. They ignore most dogs because there are few canines that actually pose a threat to a Pit Bull. As a matter of fact, if you didn't know it, you would probably think the Pit Bull wasn't that great of a fighter because it's so silly, happy and carefree. The self-confident, world-conquering bulldog carries his own weather system. He's not worried—he's happy. Why? Because he's ignorant of all the bad stuff around him? No, because he knows he can conquer whatever difficulty gets shot his way.

Pit Bulls never seem to grow old, either. They are eternal puppies. They have never heard the saying, "act your age." The old, gray, muzzled Pit Bull still thinks he's a six-month-old pup. They absolutely love to party, play and have a good time. Pit Bulls love kids. They would rather hang out with the young at heart than the refined, phony hypocrites.

Pit Bulls have a fixed grin on their faces. They exude self-confidence. When friends come over to my house, my little bulldog, Beastie, becomes the ultimate host—bathing feet, washing ears... he greets everyone. He'll catch food off his nose for you, roll over or even pull you on your roller blades if you're tired. He's is a party machine. No drugs. No booze. Beastie and all Pit Bulls are high on life. Because Pit Bulls aren't scared of anything, they can be happy in all things.

Since you are a Pit Bull, it's okay to act like a kid again. Forget this phony, pretentious, mature poodle junk. Have fun! Get free.

Pit Bulls are audacious. They're crazy. They have a zest for life. They don't test the water... they bail in. Sometimes they're absolutely reckless. Mind you, they're not stupid. Seldom will they do something that's ridiculous; nevertheless, if it looks like there's a possibility they could pull something off—you will always find them going for it, rather than holding back. As a Pit Bull, you're going to find that you're no longer timid, mousy or apologetic. Instead you're audacious, zealous, fun loving.

When you wake up in the morning, as a Pit Bull, you're ready to go. No more complaining. No more sleeping ridiculously late. You might be missing something. You might be missing a fight... an opportunity for a great dog battle. You spring out of bed. You wake ready to kick butt and take names. The bulldog's attitude is the same as Nike's—"Just Do It." Pits yell morning, noon and night, "Go for it." Pit Bulls charge into hell with a water pistol knowing that they can extinguish its flames.

> ## The fact is to do anything in the world worth doing, we must not stand back shivering and thinking of the cold and danger, but jump in and scramble through as well as we can.
>
> ~Richard Cushing

The reason why a Pit Bull is so happy and gutsy is because his name stands for:

Powerful
Individual
That
Believes
Unfailingly
Life is...
Luscious!

Everything you face, face it boldly. Rejoice in all things, even bad stuff. You know that ultimately, because you're a Pit Bull, you're going to land on top. Be happy. Be crazy. You won't survive unless you get a little crazy. Accustom yourself to do things that require guts and stamina. Tackle a big project. I recommend biting off a lot more than you can chew. Set killer goals. Go defy a Goliath. Toss a rock, in faith, at a giant. Don't be afraid of anything. Refuse to be a pouty, sad, sick and ugly Poodle. You're a handsome, confident, world-class fighter—so act like one.

Courage, it would seem, is nothing less than the power to overcome danger, misfortune, fear and injustice while continuing to affirm inwardly that life, with all it's sorrows, is good; that everything is meaningful, even if in a sense beyond our understanding, and that there is always tomorrow.

~Dorothy Thompson

5 Are You Game?

> When a dog runs at you... whistle for him.
>
> ~Henry David Thoreau

Pit Bulls are dogs that have been bred for hundreds of years to do one thing: fight other Pit Bulls. With Pit Bulls, you don't have to train them to fight... it's in their genes. It's their birthright. That's why we have to have a new birth... a new start. Because by nature, we're all whiny, selfish, weak, little Poodles. Once you experience your transition from the kingdom of Poodles to the kingdom of Pit Bulls, you'll have a new genetic makeup, and engrafted deep within your DNA is a desire and right to rule.

You know, a lot of other dogs out there seem bad... they seem tough—but when it comes to beating the Pit Bull—they're no match. That's why you have to set your sights on being like the ultimate fighting machine—the Pit Bull—if you want the ultimate out of life. The English Bull Terrier, Bull Mastiff, Husky, Wolf hybrids, Akita, Dobermans, German Sheperd, Rottweiler, etc... have all been tried against the Pit Bull and have come away devastated. Dogs that outweigh, plus stand taller than the Pit Bull, have all failed miserably once they're pitted against this dog. Pound for pound, no other breed can handle them… not even badgers or wolverines. Heck, they use Pit Bulls to capture huge bulls and wild boar! No other dog can hold a candle to the tenacity of the Pit Bull, the greatest of all dogs.

Let's look at what makes the Pit Bull such an unconquerable warrior… and what will make you an unconquerable teenager, mom, athlete, businessman or whatever else you may be.

> **Don't hit at all if it is**
>
> **honorably possible to**
>
> **avoid hitting; but**
>
> **never hit soft.**
>
> **~Theodore Roosevelt**

Most dogs don't really fight; they primarily rely on bluffing their opponent. Real life, "the pit fight," eventually finds out those who are bluffing and those who are champions.

Here's how most dogs and people fight. First, they bare their teeth... they act very serious. They try to look really scary by showing their fangs. Then, they raise the hair on the backs of their necks and backs, attempting to appear larger than they really are. After that they begin to make a lot of noise... growling, snarling, etc. Next, they might even begin to snap at their opponent and shake it. But if all those things don't work, they make a speedy, strategic withdrawal with their tail between their legs!

Isn't that how most people live? They say they're going to do something worthy... raise a great family, start a dream business, become a great athlete or musician. They show their teeth... man, do they look serious. They raise their hairs... boy, they look big and cool. They make a lot of noise about what they're going to do. Then—they even go for it and shake it a little bit. But it's all a bluff! If it doesn't work—and work soon—they are heading for the hills. They retreat. They run back to Poodleville. Back to mommy. Back to the rut and to mediocrity. Back to the silk, sissy pillow.

The Pit Bull approaches a fight in a totally different way. Pit Bulls make no threatening display. They know no bluff. They almost never bare their teeth. If their hair is raised at all, it's usually only in the first few seconds of the fight, and it's not for the sake of bluffing; it's just a natural reaction to the inward excitement generated by the fight. Pit Bulls virtually make no noise. The bulldog doesn't snap, but bites down and begins to shake the opponent releasing only to get a better hold.

Legendary strength, strong jaws and an incredibly high toleration of pain are the standard equipment for the Pit Bull. All of these are a must for successful Pit Bulls and people, but the thing that really gives the Pit its edge is his gameness. Without gameness, ability is worth nothing. Gameness is hard to keep, but essential for true success; therefore, it is priceless in its value. Gameness is the ability to never give up... never quit—regardless of the punishment taken and regardless of how tired the combatant is. Gameness is important because it intimidates all the other dogs. A truly game dog can beat a bigger and stronger dog that doesn't possess sufficient gameness. This is the most treasured quality of the Pit Bull dog.

That's why it really doesn't matter what a Pit Bull looks like. They are not show dogs. The trait that is valued is gameness. It matters very little what show dog people think about a Pit Bull. Outward appearance... perfections in coloration... head size, etc... don't figure in at all in the worth of a Pit Bull if there is not the prize trait of being game. If the dog has not the capacity to take a licking and keep on ticking—who cares if it looks good? Who cares how sharp one looks if he gets knocked out in the first round?

The trait of being game is the key to the Pit Bull's success. Gameness is the Stargate. It is what is inside of his heart that makes him the champion, the *Braveheart*, the mighty warrior. As Coach Bear Bryant said, "It's not the size of the dog in the fight that counts, but the size of the fight inside the dog." The Pit Bull's unworldly love of the battle is what gives him the edge over his competitors. This is the intimidating factor. This is what causes him to succeed.

As a Pit Bull, don't worry about what you look like… whether or not you're perfect, whatever that is. When everyone else is making noise… baring their teeth… looking cool… trying to look bigger than they really are, don't let it shame you or fool you. Remember, the empty truck makes the most noise. Rather, focus on hanging in there with your desire, your dream. Know that it doesn't matter how many rounds you lead, but whether or not you devastate those who rely on bluffing.

Courage to start and willingness to keep at it are the requisites for success.

~Alonzo Newton Benn

Beware of shallow commitments. Age and treachery will always win over youth and zeal. Don't live for show. Concern yourself with the ability to get back up again if you fall and keep at it until you conquer your desire.

Watch a man with scrutiny when his will is crossed, and his desires disappointed. The quality of spirit he reveals at that time will determine the character of the man.

~Richard T. Williams

Quick 6 Start Your Pit Bullishness.

It is a funny thing about life—
if you refuse to accept
anything but the best you very
often get it.

~W. Somerset Maugham

If you are finding yourself to be a Poodle,
but you've decided to rid your life of all
your fluff and you're ready for radical

change—here are 5 sure things that'll help you make the leap into Pit Bullhood:

1. Find Your Niche. What flicks your switch? If you could do whatever you wanted, and it was righteous and somewhat feasible—what would you do? You have got to define your passion. Take the time to figure out what stirs your heart. Pinpoint it. Write it down... and do it now. Don't play around. Pit Bulls aren't indecisive. Bulldogs don't float from being a philosopher to an army man to a secret agent to a brain surgeon. They know exactly what they want, and they don't mess with anything else.

Pit Bulls might have a few side interests, but they jam to a solid, funky, bottom-line bass note that is clear and unchanging. You must be able to spit out with absolute clarity what you are all about... that which you live for... what you want from life, personally, familially and vocationally. Define what you want, when you want it and in what quantity. If you don't—you will be a "woulda-shoulda-coulda" Poodle the rest of your life.

I care not what
your education is,
elaborate or
nothing, what your
mental caliber is,
great or small;
that man who
concentrates all
his energies of
body, mind and
soul in one
direction is a
tremendous man.
~T. Dewitt
Talmage

2. Cut The Fat. Fat will kill you. Fat is the excess baggage which is detrimental to your future progress. A good place to start is with the 50 plus hours of TV you watch a week. Get this into you: Television is an E.I.R.: Electronic Income Reducer. TV has killed more dreams and visions than crack could ever hope to. If you watch TV, let it serve you versus you, it. Watch it selectively. Watch what pushes you into greatness. Watch what is noble and beneficial (If you can find anything!). Use your time wisely.

This one thing I do.
~St. Paul

Think of how great a Pit Bull you could already be if you utilized all your past combined TV time in developing your relationships with your kids, business or personal growth. The longer the TV stays on the longer you stay a Poodle. Anyway, who wants to sit for hours watching other people live out their desires while you drink warm beer on your titanium-reinforced, duct-taped love seat in your cinder block-based trailer home?

Also, cut the fat on all non-productive relationships. Dad, quit hanging out with your going-nowhere "buddies" who resemble the cast on *King of The Hill.* Your kids miss you and need you. Mom, don't let a messed up, gossiping, sexless, needs-desperately-to-get-a-life, soap-opera-watching, *Jerry Springer*-devotee, who eternally ties up your phone line and life, rule your day. Young person, don't hang around with a Satan-worshipping punk who wears army fatigues and has so many body piercings that when he rides his dirt bike his body whistles fourteen different tunes. You must get away from kids who blow up mailboxes and who have no greater goal beyond their next keg party and goat roast. You must immediately get away from folks who want to remain Poodles. I'm not being ugly for the sake of being ugly. I firmly believe in loving thy neighbor—*but chose your neighborhood.* Get around people who have vision, great families, positive direction and avoid being a part of another person's carnage. As R.A. Dickson said, "Love your enemies just in case your friends turn out to be a bunch of bastards."

If you simply took control of TV and separated yourself from negative and smothering relationships, you would be well on your way to success.

3. Change Your Crowd. Since some of your "friends" or family could be your greatest hindrance, you might have to

make new relationships. But even if you don't have to, *make* yourself do it. Add to the repertoire of people who affect your life. I have experienced incredible personal development through hanging out with people who aren't like me. Sure, it was initially uncomfortable, but my discomfort was far greater hanging with the schleps I used to run with than the angst I temporarily went through with a new crowd.

An incredible car needs a battery that is charged by both a positive and a negative pole. Get around people who don't see things like you do... who have broader experiences. Don't inbreed, synergize. There are a lot of cool Pit Bulls out there who can really challenge and enlighten you. Go find them, and you won't stay a Poodle for long.

4. Set Killer Goals. Outsized, stretched targets will motivate you far more than

reasonable ones. Never pick a small fight. In the Bible, David challenged and killed Goliath, not his ugly sister. What challenge is it for a Pit Bull to whip a Rat Terrier?

Failure is only postponed success as long as courage "coaches" ambition. The habit of persistence is the habit of victory.

~Herbert Kaufman

Demand of yourself that which stretches you like a water-ski rope with Rush Limbaugh on the other end of it.

Don't measure your vision by that which is reachable... nor by what other people are doing. Go for the "Mission Impossible." Focus. Incite people's ridicule and use their derision to spur you on into greatness. Your success will be the sweetest revenge.

5. Live Tooth, Fang and Claw. In the process of your personal development, don't quit. It took time to get in the mess you're in, and it'll take time to get out. Yet, at the same time, don't be passive about being a Poodle. Like Ted Nugent said, "Live tooth, fang and claw." Aggressively attack the mirror. Work on your weaknesses until they've become your strengths.

Don't make a big deal over your past. It's past. Take a good look over your right shoulder... then your left... and make that the last time you look back. From now on, you're a Pit Bull. Live tooth, fang and claw and be determined to succeed.

Raising Pit Bull Children.

7

Many ideas grow better when transplanted into another mind than the one where they sprang up.

~Oliver Wendell Holmes

It seems that excellent and courageous kids are getting harder and harder to find nowadays. More and more we are seeing less and less of the scrappy little Pit Bull *Braveheart's* in our schoolyards and playgrounds. One reason we're seeing a decline of kids with Pit Bull attitudes is because Pit Bull adults are marrying folks who aren't Pit Bulls. Some Pit Bulls are actually marrying Poodles!

Marrying anything other than a Pit Bull is a stupid mistake. These bizarre unions give birth to offspring that don't carry the deep gameness that a solid union of like animals would, so we end up with a diluted, weaker specimen because of the mixtures of the different breeds.

Another reason why we're seeing a decline in Pit Bull kids is because Pit Bull parents are getting obsessed with bigger dog houses... better treadmills... fancier chains... flashier collars... hotter breaking sticks. It's not enough to give birth to a little bulldog, Pit Bull Mom and Dad, you must give it constant instruction and love.

If you don't love and discipline your kids, you seriously decrease their chances of being a champion in the arena.

Raising quality Pit Bull kids is the most important job on the planet—aside from keeping interns away from President Clinton. Just one example of the reason why parenting is so important: this world is messed up. We cannot neglect our Pit Bull kids because of our petty selfishness. If we want a better world then we must train our children well.

Here are six MUSTS to raising quality Pit Bull children:

1. A Pit Bull sire and dam must love their pups. I'm not just talking about emotionally, but sacrificially. Make sure you hang out with your kids more than you do your yahoo friends. Take them on dates. Take then hunting and fishing or

wherever you like to go. Get them into sports or something else constructive. Get involved in their world, and let them be involved in yours. Communicate with

them. Give them more than just cash and a casa. Give them your time and attention.

2. Bless your Pit Bull pups. Continually speak that which inspires them. Help your pups realize their purpose and destiny.

Give them hope. Teach them primary greatness such as integrity, character, faith, passion and tenacity. Mom and Dad, your little pup is a blank canvas upon which you can paint a *Monet* or a *Beavis and Butthead*... I suggest the former.

3. Pray for your pups. There is incredible power in prayer. This is not a light thing. All the great Biblical patriarchs prayed for their pups and subsequently produced a greater little bulldog. Invoke God's help for yours and your little ones' well being. Pray for their spiritual, mental, physical and financial prosperity. PRAY AGAINST ALL TEMPTATIONS TO BE A POODLE. This is serious business raising Pit Bulls, and prayer figures in greatly to quality formation. Also, find a good Pit Bull-type church (If you're having trouble finding one, contact my office for U.S., South African and European listings).

4. Discipline your bulldogs. Pit Bulls need discipline. They need a strong chain or cable system. If not, they are highly likely to get into serious trouble. Never beat your pup or verbally abuse it. That's stupid, and if you do that, *you* need to be put down. It's okay to be very firm, but not in anger— rather in principle, with tough love. Make sure all your discipline is redemptive, not punitive.

5. Give your puppies instruction. Discipline not only entails correction, but also instruction. Don't just blather on about what is wrong and focus on the negative, but show them what's right. Walk the talk, Pit Bull Mom and Dad. You can't expect them not to be a Poodle when they see you being one. Pit Bull see. Pit Bull do. Instruction is caught, not taught. The impartation of instruction comes via the avenue of direct contact and observation. If you don't want your pups to be Boy George-Michael Jackson-

Poodle freaks, then you must hang out with them. Read them books that inspire them to independent thinking, action and leadership.

6. Be an available source of supply for your puppies' needs. Spiritually, socially, physically, financially and mentally—be their provider, protector and hero. Make sure you have an arsenal of wisdom, tools and whatever else they need to help them as they prepare to scratch in the pit of life. There will come a time when this particular stage will phase out, but make sure you're there during this crucial aspect of development.

Your Pit Bull son or daughter has unlimited potential for greatness. The purpose of your leadership is not to have them serve you, but rather you them. Help them... inspire them to discover, develop and become what God has destined them to be. Provide every opportunity possible for them to find, follow and finish their unique courses in life. Set them up, then set them free to be great Pit Bulls. Don't keep them in your doghouse. Make them independent, eternal scrappers. And finally, realize that just because you're a Pit Bull doesn't mean you're a success... not until you have raised a greater successor—your pups. Make sure you are there to cause your kids to excel.

The Pit Bull Christian.

"God has not given you a spirit of fear, but of power, love and a sound mind."

2 Timothy 1.7.

When one thinks of a Christian today, one usually thinks of a weak, out-of-shape, non-productive, spineless, complaining, pink-haired Poodle. Courage, brain cells and heroism are on the endangered species list as far as most churches go. What the church presently is, she was never intended to become. God intended every believer to be a Pit Bull-Christian who smashes darkness, evil and ignorance and brings life, light and healing to our great planet.

Every *true* Christian is a Pit Bull-Christian. A Christian without a Pit Bull Attitude is a Poodle-Christian. What a terrible thought... being a Poodle-Christian. A Pit Bull-Christian is a hero... a champ... braver than the bravest. Pit Bull-Christians laugh at difficulties, disease, danger and death. Those who don't have this attitude are Poodle-Christians. Poodles run to the air-conditioned doghouse when it gets hot. Sweetie Poodle-

Christians might lose the curl in their hair if they get too close to the flame. The heat has also been known to take the nail polish off their nails. And an occasional wild flame has caught many a pink ribbon on fire.

Poodle-Christians live in the Church instead of going into the world.

Poodle-Christians say they love God but deny him with their deeds.

Poodle-Christians hear the word of God every Sunday, but they don't do it.

When the Poodle-Christian hears the call to duty... he gets a tummy ache. The call to battle always finds the Poodle-Christian busy with other Poodles at covered-dish dinners. Poodle-Christians don't like to get dirty doing the practical, tough work of obeying God—but they love poetry. Here's one of their favorite poems:

Oh how I love the Pastor who tickles my ears.
Come to me, thou prophet of peace, and
tell me what I want to hear.
Tell me of goodies, blessings and treasures
abounding just for me.
As I hide in the church and avoid the suffering.

Why be so serious?
Why take so much pain?
Have not you learned from those around it's
all just fun and games?

It's time to create a new breed of believers. No more Poodles... just Pit Bulls. The scripture condemns Poodle-

Christians but cheers the Pit Bull-believers. It's time to look at the scripture through the eyes of the Pit Bull. So, put on your Bad-Boy Ray Bans, and let's check out a few heroes in the scripture. You don't have to look very hard to find Bulldogs here.

Noah. He preached and lived righteously when the rest of the world was wicked. He feared God when it wasn't popular. He obeyed God when everyone mocked him. And only he and his family survived the flood when it came upon the earth. Noah got the last laugh… because Noah was a Pit Bull.

Abraham. At 75 years old this Pit Bull left everything and followed God. Radical. With 318 men, this old Bulldog whipped the combined armies of five great kings. Not too shabby for a farmer. His secret? He was a Pit Bull who lived to please his Master.

Jacob. Old Jake didn't like himself nor his situation too much, so one night he bit down on the angel of God and with a strong jaw-lock he muttered, "I won't let you go until you *make me a Pit Bull!*" (author's translation).

Joseph. Joe was a teenage Pit Bull when he first appeared in scripture. He had a vision that made his brothers jealous (They were Poodles. Poodles are always jealous.), so his brothers sold him into slavery. For years Joseph was abused, misunderstood and lied about. But because he was a Pit Bull, he ultimately rose out of obscurity to a place of dominion. What a dude... what a Pit Bull!

Moses. Moses could have easily been a Poodle. He was heir to Pharaoh's throne. But he didn't want it. Why? He had Pit Bull blood in him, which caused him to blow off Egypt, silk pajamas and other Poodle paraphernalia and instead suffer hardships with the people of God. It took 40 years for his vision to come to pass. *Forty years.* Talk about gameness! Talk about being a Pit Bull. Most Christians won't wait 40 days, much less 40 years. But Moses did. That's why we read about him centuries later.

Joshua and Caleb. A couple of 85-year-old wild dogs who put up one hellacious fight and, along with a group of radical warriors, obtained the Promised Land. Put that in your pipe and smoke it. They weren't concerned with their age. They didn't know they were supposed to retire. They couldn't retire even if they wanted to, because, you see… they were Pit Bulls.

David. David was a teenage Pit Bull, also. He didn't go to *watch* the battle, he went to *fight* the battle. He ran to the front. He did what all the Mature, sensible Poodle-soldiers couldn't do—kill Goliath.

He said he would kill the Philistine, and he did kill the Philistine... single handedly. Crazy, audacious, teenage Pit Bull material.

John the Baptist. He wasn't a Poodle. He made all of Israel mad... from the president to the preachers. He made all the Poodles squirm. John wore camel's hair and ate locusts (now that's Pit Bull attire and diet). Jesus said of John, "When you went out into the wilderness, what did you go out there to see? A poodle? I say you went out to see a Pit Bull—and one who is more than a Pit Bull. John was the greatest among Pit Bulls" (author's translation).

The Apostle Paul. Talk about a radical Pit Bull. Satan took a few weeks vacation after this bulldog was killed. Paul was called a "fool" and "mad" because of his unstoppable Pit Bull zeal. A top notch theologian, who didn't live in seminary— but took his revelation out of the church and into the pit and came out converting whole cities. This game rascal took incredible abuse and yet never lost his joy. He was a disaster to Satan's kingdom. He finally caused so much trouble hell had no recourse but to cut his head off. God help us to be one fourth of the Pit Bull Paul was.

Then you have the Poodle "believers." False, spurious, eternal rejects from God's kingdom, donning pink hair and carrying a wheel barrow load of excuses.

Rueben. He was a Poodle. He had great intentions... serious heart resolves. But at the end of the day, he would rather sit and listen to shepherds play songs rather than get into the fray. He would rather squat on the sidelines of life than be on the playing field.

Meroz. The people of this city were Poodles, as well. Little, frilly nothings

They, too, would rather go to conferences and Christian concerts than attempt to bring biblical solutions to modern problems. A fat, overfed people who were ultimately cursed of God.

Demas. He used to hang out with the old warrior Paul, but he left when things got tough. He decided he would rather settle for what Poodles have—boring mediocrity—than what the Pit Bulls enjoy—namely, the fight.

Mark. He had to deal with being a Poodle, too. He went out with Pit Bull Paul, but when then stones started flying and the bones started cracking... he was out of there like a boot-legger out of Alabama on a Saturday night. After that display of Poodleness, Paul would have nothing to do with him. Pit Bulls don't hang around with Poodles. Only later, after Mark experienced a radical transformation into a Pit Bull did Paul regard him as profitable.

One thing that would help the Church immensely would be if the pastors would stop breeding for show and instead breed for courage. Quit encouraging people to be dependent, spiritless Poodles. Don't produce what you or your denomination necessarily likes. Produce something that is effective... that can bring Christ's healing to a sin-ravaged world.

Christians are so quick to give up. So ready for Jesus to come rescue them. This is Pathetic. Because of our aversion to fight the good fight of faith, our society has become increasingly decadent as we content ourselves with our Sunday morning dog shows.

May God give us an unworldly love for spiritual conflict. May God give us deep gameness, so that no matter what demons we face—we will not be deterred from this high and lofty call. Oh, that there would be a people who long for the battle

instead of a place of ease inside of Christian Disneyland. May God make us all into that which He is not ashamed of... Pit Bull Christians.

Dealing With Poodles' Criticism.

Beware out there if you have decided that you're going to be a Pit Bull. You'll be attacked by rabid Poodles quicker than a silk blouse marked down to $2.99 at a Wal-Mart Manager's Day Sale. Poodles hate it when their buddies leave them in order

> **We should not forget that our tradition is one of protest and revolt, and it is stultifying to celebrate the rebels of the past... while we silence the rebels of the present.**
>
> ~Henry Steele Commager

to become a Pit Bull. They hate it when you no longer go to their beauty parlors. They hate it when they see you leave them in their comfort zone, a/c-regulated environments and launch out on your own to conquer your dream...to get in the pit and test your skills.

Get ready for the Poodles to assault you for your vision and your dream. The reason why they attack you is because you shame them. By your going for it, actually living out your passion, you remind them of what wusses they are... what Poodles they have become.

Poodles will try to force their opinions on you... opinions of why you should be like them and stay in their comfortable, safe and boring dog houses. Don't listen to the Poodles' opinions. Who wants to listen to some pale-skinned Poodle... some unqualified blowhard who has convinced himself that his uninformed Poodle opinion is somehow relevant to Pit Bull issues concerning our lives and our desires?

Know this, all Pit Bull's: Poodles don't know squat. Poodles haven't done squat. They are flakes who have accomplished nothing. Do not listen to them, or you will become like them. Have this Pit Bull Attitude: "If you can't run your own life, Ms. Poodle, I certainly won't let you run mine." Let the Poodle's mockery and ridicule motivate you. Your success will be your greatest revenge. Be radical for your vision and dream to such an extent that you leave the Poodles behind, choking in your dust. Hey, Poodle—Eat my dust!

Let me help all you young Pit Bulls who are deciding to step away from the Poodles and actually do something with your lives. Just Do It. Get it on. Direction

Its name is
Public Opinion.
It is held in
reverence. It
settles
everything.
Some think it is
the voice of God.
Loyalty to
petrified opinion
never yet broke
a chain
or freed a
human soul.

~**Mark Twain**

comes with motion. Get into motion with your purpose and desire and get away from puny, critical, beady-eyed Fi-Fi's. Do not be sidelined by some spiteful crank heaping scorn on everything he sees. Your life is between you and God. Not you and an anemic Poodle. Live by the convictions you have in your heart.

Why should you—a great Pit Bull—be bothered by the slings and arrows of Poodles whom you should not give one-tenth of a flip about? Why should you give

s o m e Poodle the power over whether or not you feel good about yourself and your unique purpose in life?

There are five things you must remember about Poodle critics:

1. Critics are like eunuchs in a harem. They're there every night. They see it done every night. They see how it should be done every night. But they can't do it themselves.

—Brendan Behan

2. Any fool can criticize, and most of them do.

—C. Garbett

3. Don't pay attention to critics—don't even ignore them.

—Samuel Goldwyn

4. Critics are a dissembling, contemptible race of men. Asking a player what he feels about critics is like asking a lamppost what it feels about dogs.

—John Osborne

5. To escape criticism—do nothing, say nothing, be nothing.

—Elbert Hubbard

I know I've been hard on the Poodles who criticize us Pit Bulls. But you know what? I can honestly say I love my enemies who give me a hard time. I love every bone in their heads.

Remember this, Pit Bulls: The most important critic is *time.*

Time is on the Pit Bull's side... yes it is.

You may talk of the tyranny of Nero and Tiberius; but the real tyranny is the tyranny of your next door neighbor. Public opinion is a permeating influence, and it exacts obedience to itself; it requires us to think other men's thoughts, to speak other men's words, to follow other men's habits.

~Walter Bagehot

Losing A Roll: Surviving Defeat.

10

> **We've been
> surrounded and
> battered by trouble,
> but we're not
> demoralized... we
> have been thrown
> down, but we haven't
> broken.**
>
> ~St. Paul's Second Letter to
> the Corinthians

Probably one of the most difficult things for a Pit Bull to experience is a defeat. It's difficult for a bulldog to experience this because he's a conqueror... a success... a champion. But, just because you fail in something, all is not lost. Pit dog men will often test their dogs with a practice roll (a short fight) before they actually pit them in a true contest with a game dog. The purpose of the roll is to see how the dogs fare in a small skirmish. Sometimes the young, inexperienced dog will take some serious blows. This can look like a failure or a weakness to the undiscerning eye, but great dog men know there is no other way to bring out the fight in a dog than to let it get a taste of the action, and if need be— experience a good whipping.

People who are bent on success will find themselves getting slam-dunked more often than apple fritters do at the Dunkin Donuts located next to the Boston Police Department. Therefore, you must understand that if you want the ultimate out of life, you're going to face the ultimate challenges in order to get it. If your dream is truly noble and worthy, it will guarantee tremendous resistance. If your accomplishment can be easily gained then you need to reconsider the greatness of your goals. Great Pit Bulls become great because they are pitted against *the creme de le creme* of fighting dogs and come out the champs. So expect intense internal and external pressures.

I get knocked down, but I get up again... Ain't nothing gonna keep me down.

~Chumbawamba

Even though you're an awesome little bulldog, that doesn't guarantee you're going to win every battle. There are serious dogs out there that love to punish the new dogs on the block. This is nothing to get discouraged about. If you play a loss right, you can learn a great deal and be better prepared for the next battle. If you fail to learn, then you're in for another booty-kicking.

One thing that a loss brings is that gross, yucky feeling of having been defeated, which attacks your feelings of self-worth as a Pit Bull. You don't feel like a champ... you feel like a chump. You begin to lose your Pit Bull Attitude. Your confidence and determination levels begin to sink really low. You begin to think how easy it was when you were a Poodle, and you didn't have to put up with this junk. You're even tempted to get your hair permed, run back home to mommy and get your toenails painted pink. You even put that pink ribbon back on your forehead when no one was looking. STOP THAT IMMEDIATELY. QUIT BEING A VICTIM.

You're a Pit Bull, man—so act like one. Just because you have suffered loss doesn't mean you have ceased to be a

I love the man who can smile in trouble, who can gather strength from distress and grow brave by reflection. 'Tis the business of little minds to shrink, but he whose heart is firm, and whose conscience approves his conduct, will pursue his principles unto death. ~Thomas Paine champion. Cry if it's necessary. Lick your wounds, if need be. But don't do it for long, or you'll find a foul, wicked, Poodle-quitting spirit begin to ooze all over your Pit Bull Attitude.

When you do lose a battle, expect the Poodles to come out of the woodwork to mock you saying, "I told you so"... "You're

never gonna make it"… yada yada yada. The reason why your failure incites their wrath is because your vision shames their lack of ambition and their love of the comfort zone. Your success causes them to suffer the most. When you excel, they hate it. So naturally, you should expect their yapping when you blow it. Don't sweat it. They're Poodles. They're nothing. If your actions and vision don't challenge them, then you're simply striving for the insignificant.

If you have taken a beating, and you're presently in the doghouse bleeding, shaken and disillusioned, realize that you still can become great if you learn from your loss. So, walk out of your doghouse… think about what happened… how and why you got bested… shake the dust off… and yell at the top of your lungs, **"I am a Pit Bull! The ultimate fighting machine. I am determined to get back up and get into the battle. I am not going to** play the victim. I'm not going to be a Poodle. I'm a Pit dog determined to get my desires!"

Don't let your passion die out just because you got smashed. Ignite now, the fire of your desires. Don't let your vision smolder. Whip it back up into the flame of a blow torch—for as long as a Pit Bull breathes, there is still hope.

Be stirring as the time, be fire with fire, threaten the threatener and outface the brow of bragging horror; so shall inferior eyes, who borrow their behaviors from the great, grow great by your example and put on the dauntless spirit of resolution.

~**William Shakespeare**

Doug Giles is an outstanding man of God with a burning desire to see today's youth maximize their potential and play a positive and constructive part in the society in which they live. He is a man of integrity and someone who will be an excellent role model for young people.

Paul Daniel, Founder/President
His People Christian Ministries
Cape Town, South Africa

Doug Giles

about the author

When nations, cities, communities, marriages, relationships, churches and individuals lose their sense of purpose, then confusion, frustration, discouragement and destruction begin to take control.

This is evident in every facet of our world. The lack of purpose leads to the loss of values, morals and convictions, which are what build strong families, secure communities, healthy cities and prosperous nations. Most people want to know the answer to the question, "Why am I here?" Doug Giles wants to aid people in answering that question. He has given his life to help people, especially young adults, find, follow and finish the destiny in each of their lives.

But things were different several years ago. He was going nowhere fast...

"Doug is stirring, confrontational, challenging and equipping. We have had many speakers at our church, but few who have had the impact that Doug has had with my people. His passion is to raise up a generation of constructive world-changers."
Steve Pauwels
Senior Pastor
Living Way Church, Londonderry, New Hampshire

> "Doug's passion, both spiritual and intellectual, is to see people connected to a God of love, life and purpose. His ministry is life giving and full of hope. He is a man of humor, wit and relevance. I commend him to you happily and unreservedly."
>
> Andrew Shearman, President
> Reformation International
> San Antonio, Texas

A drug user from the age of twelve. Doug was arrested at sixteen for burglary and kicked out of both high school and college. By age twenty-one he found himself with as much sense of direction as a busted compass. Ready to check out of the game of life, Doug called on God, and thankfully He was accepting calls that day.

While living in Texas, he graduated from college with a Bachelor of Fine Arts degree, married and had

> Doug has been a real encouragement to me personally and to my family. Doug's desire for excellence in his personal and professional life has been a great influence on our family to move beyond the status quo. Doug has been a second dad to my three sons, moving them towards excellence in their education and hobbies. You'll break new ground with Doug."
>
> Captain Cameron Hitchcock
> American Airlines,
> West Palm Beach, Florida

two daughters. Doug ran a successful business, and in his spare time, began speaking in prisons, detention centers, churches and nightclubs. He then established a church in west Texas and was aired daily on a 30 minute radio program. Since then his ministry has extended internationally into England, Mexico, Holland and South Africa.

Doug has authored two books, has several others in progress and is completing his Masters degree in Divinity. He is also pioneering a new church in Miami, Florida.

Doug knows firsthand what it is to have everything stacked against you, but he also knows that by having a realization of your true destiny you can live out the life of your dreams...

"I have observed Doug and his work for over ten years, and he has a proven track record of leading people out of destructive life-styles and into freedom, healing and purpose. It is rare to find a young man with his wisdom, creativity and depth. Doug will inspire all who hear him to excellence, diligence, independent thinking and community service. I anticipate his continuous and powerful influence to impact a wayward generation."

Dr. Mel Winger, El Shaddai Church
Guatemala City, Guatemala

For speaking engagements, seminars or consultation, contact:

Doug Giles
P.O. Box 800554
Aventura, FL 33280
Tel: 305.937.3774
www.pitbullattitude.com